BLUEPRINT

FOR

ENERGY EFFICIENT

BUILDINGS

Unlocking Insultion Secrets for Modern Indin Buildings

BLUEPRINT

FOR

ENERGY EFFICIENT

BUILDINGS

Unlocking Insultion Secrets for Modern Indin Buildings

VISHAL RUSTAGI

Worldwide Published by

Pendown Press

PENDOWN PRESS LLP

An ISO 9001 & ISO 14001 Certified Co.,

Regd. Office: 3767A, Kanhaiya Nagar,

Tri Nagar, Delhi-110035

Ph.: 8180886000, 9650072927, 8595249536

E-mail: info@pendownpress.com

Branch Office: 1A/2A, 20, Hari Sadan, Ansari Road,

Daryaganj, New Delhi-110002

Ph.: 011-45794768

Website: PendownPress.com

First Edition: 2023

Price: ₹299/-

ISBN: 978-93-5554-892-4

Layout and Cover Designed by Pendown Graphics Team
Printed and Bound in India by Thomson Press India Ltd.

TABLE OF CONTENTS

ABOUT THIS BOOK

Welcome to **"Blueprint for Energy Efficient Buildings"** In the world of construction and environmental awareness, insulation is crucial. Whether you're an architect, builder, contractor, PMC or a homeowner, this guide will help you navigate the world of insulation materials. Whether you're an architect, a DIY enthusiast, or a homeowner, this guide will help you navigate the world of insulation materials.

In these pages, we explain the basics of insulation, the different materials available, and their characteristics. We also discuss the environmental impact of insulation and the need for eco-friendly options.

This book is more than a manual; it's a journey through insulation, helping you make informed choices for your comfort, budget, and the environment. Whether you want to save on energy bills, improve indoor comfort, or go green, this guide has the answers.

Join us on this educational adventure to discover the secrets, benefits, and challenges of insulation materials. By the end, you'll be well-prepared to make the right choices and create cozy, energy-efficient spaces.

Get ready for a transformative journey as we explore the world of building insulation materials, where knowledge is your best tool.

ACKNOWLEDGEMENTS

I always dreamed of writing a book, but it seemed like a big challenge. I want to thank the many people who supported me in my life journey and helped me complete my first book. This book represents almost 20 years of learning and experience, and it wouldn't have happened without the guidance and encouragement of many.

Thanks to all who walked with me on my life path.

Firstly, thanks to my parents for giving me life and teaching me values that make me a good person. Their upbringing enables me to live my purpose, and this book is a part of that.

A big thank you to my mentor, Akshar Yadav, who changed how I see things and helped me discover my true potential. Special thanks to my wife Sweety, daughter Yashita, and son Rayansh for bringing joy to my life.

The publication of this book would not have been possible without the support of Dinesh Verma and his wonderful team at Pendown Press.

I am thankful to Harsh Bansal (Unity Group) for having trust in me and giving me my first insulation work. Harsh ji is one of the few builders I have come across who prioritizes quality above price.

I appreciate Sanjeev Gupta and Amit Gupta (Girdhari Lal Construction - government civil contractors) for their valuable suggestions. They are truly knowledgeable and genuine individuals.

I am thankful to my friend Dinesh Verma, CEO, Pendown Press and his team for their support and suggestions throughout the creative process.

MY STORY

Failures are like stepping stones on the path to knowledge. When we stumble and fall, it's our curiosity that keeps us going. It's in the face of defeat that our curiosity awakens, asking, "Why did this happen? What could I do differently?" We learn from these questions and find new insights. Each failure is like a puzzle, a challenge that helps us grow stronger and wiser.

I come from a small town called Sirsa in Haryana, and I completed my graduation at Kurukshetra University. I've always been eager to learn new things and meet new people. After graduation, I got married to my dear wife, Sweety Rustagi, and initially joined my family's jewelry business. However, I found the job uninteresting and requested my grandfather's support to start a new business. With his help, I ventured into the mobile phone and glass film business. During this time, God blessed us with a lovely angel, Yashita.

As Yashita grew, I explored new opportunities, learning about modular kitchens and water treatment businesses in Delhi and adding them to my business. While my business was doing well, I realized that there was limited room for growth in small towns. So, I decided to hand over the business to my brother and moved to Delhi to establish it there.

In a few months, I understand that starting a business from scratch in a big city like Delhi was a tough challenge. At times,

I felt like giving up, but my wife and mother provided unwavering support. In my first year, I received support from my uncles and cousins. During this time, I started a water treatment business, and my family moved to Delhi. I also ventured into an interior contracting business in partnership, which initially performed well but suffered significant losses in a project. To make ends meet, I entered a partnership with my cousin's epoxy flooring business. During this time, my wife and I were blessed with a son named Rayansh. These years were the toughest time of my life, and I struggled to pay my flat rent and school fees for my kids.

Here, I'd like to mention that the movie "3 Idiots" played a life-changing role in my journey. After watching it multiple times, I gathered the courage to face one of the toughest challenges of my life. Starting a new business, my friend Vikram Sahoo introduced me to Mr. Rajeev Tyagi, the regional director of BASF India Ltd. Despite the difficulty in obtaining a dealer code from BASF, Tyagi Sir offered me a challenging project, which I had never done before. It involved a significant amount of material, and the applicators had left due to the dangerous nature of the job. I accepted this challenge and not only completed the project but also earned a good profit from it.

In the following years, I faced and overcame various challenging projects, thanks to my association with BASF. I learned that as a business owner, it's essential to keep up with changing technology. I began receiving training in concrete technology, flooring, and admixtures from various locations in India. In 2014, I reached another milestone by starting my private limited company and entering the world of waterproofing and insulation. Through my ability to handle challenging projects, I was entrusted with a high-pressure polyurea waterproofing project at upcoming underground metro stations, considered one of the most prestigious and demanding waterproofing jobs in India. My team and I not only took on the job but also completed it to the site's requirements. Our performance led to more station projects and recognition as one of the top-performing agencies in India at BASF's annual conference.

During this time, I attended seminars on green buildings and technologies, which sparked my interest in new technologies for thermal insulation in buildings. As a supporter of green products, I began gaining knowledge in this field and learning about thermal insulation for buildings.

From 2014 to 2023, my company executed more than 40 lakh square feet of waterproofing and insulation on prestigious Indian projects, including IIT Delhi, IIT Bhubaneswar, IIT Durg, Sanjay Gandhi Cancer Hospital, Lucknow, IOCL Refineries, AIIMS Delhi, ITC, and DLF, among others. I not only completed these projects but also trained over 40 people and students, including those in prestigious institutes like IIT Delhi. Recently, our company was nominated as one of the top 10 companies in India, and a LinkedIn survey recognized us as one of the top 20 companies engaged in thermal insulation in 2023. I was elected as the Vice President (North) of the "Waterproofers Association of India" in 2023.

By 2022, I realized that there was a significant gap in the construction industry concerning insulation products and techniques. It surprised me that many builders, architects, consultants, and homeowners were still using outdated methods for insulation, which were less effective, expensive, and challenging to execute. I decided to increase my knowledge and began working to educate people, especially those in the construction industry, about the importance of insulation in energy savings and comfortable living.

During my journey, I met my mentor, Akshar Yadav, who inspired me to share my thoughts and knowledge in the form of a book to spread awareness on a larger scale.

WHY THIS BOOK (MCB)

In my previous work, I noticed a big problem in construction and sustainability. Many people who own buildings don't know enough about this topic, which can cause problems for construction and sustainability efforts. To fix this issue, I decided to write a book to help people learn more.

I also saw that the construction and sustainability industry has a lot of complicated words and terms that can be hard to understand, especially for beginners. In my book, I've made it my mission to explain these complex terms in a way that's easy to understand. This book is a helpful resource for anyone who wants to share their knowledge, promote energy efficiency, and provide practical advice to a wide audience.

Chapter 1

UNDERSTANDING THE BASICS OF INSULATION

Insulation is used to reduce the transfer of heat between two environments, usually the interior and exterior of a building. The primary purpose is to minimize heat loss in cold climates and heat gain in warm climates, improving energy efficiency and maintaining comfortable indoor temperatures. It is like a protective shield for buildings. It keeps the cold out in winter and the heat out in summer. Its main job is to help us use less energy for heating and cooling, which saves money and helps the environment.

In cold weather, insulation keeps the warmth inside, reducing the need for heating. In hot weather, it prevents too much heat from coming in, reducing the need for air conditioning. This not only makes our indoor spaces more comfortable but also lowers our energy bills and reduces greenhouse gas emissions, which is good for the planet. So, insulation is a vital part of efficient and eco-friendly construction.

Insulation works by impeding the three main modes of heat transfer:

1. **Conduction:** This is the transfer of heat through direct contact between materials. Insulation materials are poor conductors of heat, meaning they don't allow heat to flow easily through them. This property helps reduce the transfer of heat between different temperature zones. In cold weather, insulation prevents the warmth inside a building from escaping, and in hot weather, it prevents external heat from entering. Insulation materials like fiberglass, foam board, or cellulose contain tiny air pockets that trap heat and minimize its conduction.

   For instance, during the winter, fiberglass insulation in the walls of a house slows down the transfer of heat from the warm indoor air to the cold outdoor air, keeping the interior comfortably warm.

2. **Convection:** Convection involves the movement of heat through fluids. This is crucial in preventing the circulation of warm air in summer or cold air in winter, helping to maintain a consistent indoor temperature. Insulation materials are designed to reduce convective heat transfer by trapping air within their structure. Air is a poor conductor of heat, so materials with air pockets or fibers are effective at reducing convective heat flow.

   A good example is attic insulation. When you insulate your attic, it prevents warm air from rising and escaping through the roof, reducing the convection of heat from the living spaces to the outdoors. In hot weather, it also keeps hot air from entering the living areas.

3. **Radiation:** Radiation is the transfer of heat through electromagnetic waves. This is particularly important in

hot climates, where insulation can prevent the absorption of heat from the sun, keeping indoor spaces cooler. Insulation materials with reflective surfaces, such as foil or metallized films, can reflect radiant heat away from the building, reducing the heat gain or loss.

In regions with scorching summers, a radiant barrier may be installed in the attic to reflect the sun's heat away from the living space. It prevents the roof from absorbing excessive heat and radiating it downward, thus keeping the indoors cooler.

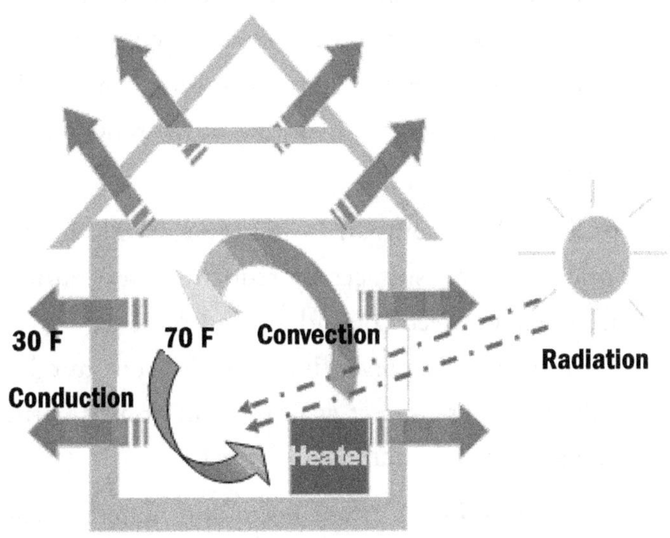

Benefits of Thermal Insulation

1. **Energy Efficiency:** One of the primary benefits of thermal insulation is improved energy efficiency. By reducing heat transfer through the building envelope, insulation helps to maintain desired indoor temperatures

with less reliance on heating and cooling systems. This leads to lower energy consumption and reduced utility bills.

2. **Reduced Heating and Cooling Costs:** Insulation minimizes heat loss during colder months and heat gain during warmer months, resulting in reduced heating and cooling needs. This translates to lower energy costs and long-term savings for building owners and occupants.

3. **Enhanced Comfort:** Properly insulated buildings offer increased comfort for occupants. Insulation helps to stabilize indoor temperatures, reduce temperature variations, and prevent drafts. It creates a more pleasant and consistent living or working environment throughout the year.

4. **Condensation Control:** Insulation can help control condensation on surfaces by reducing temperature differences between the indoor and outdoor environments. By preventing excessive moisture buildup, insulation helps protect against mold growth, structural damage, and potential health issues.

5. **Noise Reduction:** Certain insulation materials, such as mineral wool or foam, also provide sound insulation properties. They can help reduce noise transmission from outside sources or between different areas within a building, improving acoustical comfort.

6. **Environmental Benefits:** By reducing energy consumption, thermal insulation contributes to a lower carbon footprint and decreased greenhouse gas emissions

associated with heating and cooling systems. It supports sustainable building practices and environmental conservation.

7. **Longevity and Durability:** Insulation can help protect the building envelope by minimizing temperature-related expansion and contraction, which can lead to structural damage over time. It can also provide additional fire resistance, moisture resistance, and pest resistance, contributing to the longevity and durability of the building.

8. **Improved Building Value:** Buildings with good thermal insulation and energy efficiency ratings tend to have higher market value. Insulation upgrades can be seen as an investment that enhances the property's desirability and potential resale or rental value.

It's important to know that the advantages of insulation can change based on factors like the weather, how the building is made, the kind of insulation used, how well it's put in, and how it's taken care of. To get the best results, it's a good idea to talk to experts and follow local building rules.

Chapter 2

WHY IS INSULATION IMPORTANT

Insulation is a fundamental component of any building or structure, playing a crucial role in maintaining comfort, energy efficiency, and environmental sustainability. A well-insulated and well-designed home provides year-round comfort, cutting cooling and heating bills, and reducing greenhouse gas emissions. In this section, we will discuss why insulation is essential and explore the various reasons why it should be a priority for homeowners, businesses, and builders.

1. **Energy Efficiency:** Effective insulation acts as a thermal barrier, preventing the transfer of heat between the interior and exterior of a building. This barrier reduces the need for excessive heating in cold weather and cooling in hot weather. By keeping indoor temperatures stable, insulation significantly contributes to energy efficiency, which, in turn, reduces energy consumption and lowers utility bills.

2. **Cost Savings:** Improved energy efficiency resulting from proper insulation can lead to substantial cost savings over time. Reduced energy consumption translates to lower heating and cooling costs, making insulation a wise

investment for homeowners and businesses. The initial cost of insulating a building can often be recouped through these long-term savings.

3. **Enhanced Comfort:** Insulation helps maintain consistent indoor temperatures, creating a more comfortable and livable environment. In the winter, it keeps the cold out, and in the summer, it keeps the heat at bay. This consistent temperature control ensures that occupants remain comfortable year-round, without the need for constant adjustments to thermostats.

4. **Environmental Benefits:** Proper insulation not only benefits your wallet but also the environment. By reducing energy consumption, insulation minimizes the carbon footprint associated with heating and cooling systems. It is a sustainable choice that aligns with the principles of responsible energy use and can contribute to a lower overall environmental impact.

5. **Soundproofing:** In addition to thermal benefits, insulation also plays a significant role in soundproofing. It can help reduce noise transmission from outside sources and between different areas of a building. This is especially important in homes, offices, and commercial spaces where peace and privacy are desired.

6. **Structural Protection:** Insulation can contribute to the longevity and durability of a building. It helps prevent issues like condensation and moisture buildup, which can lead to structural damage, mold growth, and decreased indoor air quality. Insulation acts as a protective barrier against these threats.

7. **Compliance with Building Codes:** Many building codes and regulations require a certain level of insulation to be installed in new construction and renovations. Failing to meet these standards can result in non-compliance issues and may affect the resale value of a property.

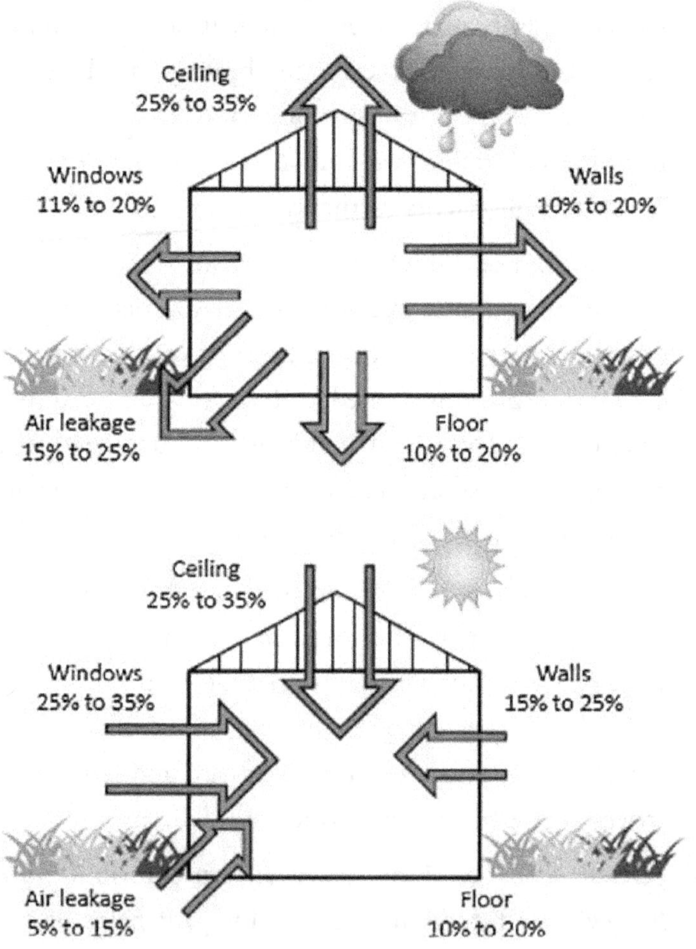

Typical heat losses and gains without insulation in a temperate climate
Source: SEAV (2002), updated in Energy Smart Housing Manual (2018)

Insulation acts as a barrier to heat flow and is essential for keeping your home warm in winter and cool in summer. It is essential for a comfortable, energy-efficient building. It saves money on energy bills, reduces environmental impact, and makes indoor spaces pleasant. Whether you own a home or a business, understanding insulation's importance is the key to creating a better, more eco-friendly, and comfortable place to live or work.

Chapter 3

TYPES OF INSULATION (BEING USED IN INDIA IN BUILDINGS)

Building insulation refers to materials or techniques used to reduce heat transfer and control temperature fluctuations within a building. It is installed in various parts of a building, such as walls, roofs, floors, and ceilings, to minimize the flow of heat between the interior and exterior environments. The primary purpose of insulation is to enhance energy efficiency, reduce heating and cooling costs, and improve occupant comfort.

Insulation works by slowing down the movement of heat through conduction, convection, and radiation. Conduction is the transfer of heat through solid materials, while convection is the movement of heat through fluids (air or liquid).

Understanding R-Value (Thermal Resistance Value)

R-Value, or thermal resistance value, is a measure of how effective insulation is at preventing heat transfer. A higher R-Value indicates better insulation, as it means the material can resist the flow of heat more effectively. This value is used to compare different insulation materials and helps in determining the right insulation for a particular application and climate conditions. The goal is to select insulation with an appropriate R-Value to maintain comfort and energy efficiency in buildings. Insulation materials are selected based on their thermal resistance Common insulation materials & methods include:

1. **Brick Bat Coba:** Brick bat coba, also known as brick bat lime terracing, is a traditional Indian method of roof insulation. It involves applying a layer of broken clay bricks (brickbats) mixed with lime mortar or cementitious material on the roof surface. This technique provides both insulation and waterproofing, making it a cost-effective choice for hot and rainy climates.

2. **Mud Phuska:** Mud phuska is another traditional method of roof insulation. It involves applying a mixture of mud, straw, and locally available materials to the roof surface. This natural and sustainable approach offers thermal insulation, keeping indoor spaces cooler in hot weather and warmer in cold weather.

3. **Fiberglass:** Fiberglass insulation is made from tiny glass fibers and is commonly used in various forms such as loose-fill, batts, or rolls. It is known for its affordability and effectiveness at trapping air and reducing heat transfer, making it a popular choice for insulating walls, ceilings, and floors.

4. **Mineral Wool:** Similar to fiberglass, mineral wool insulation is made from rock or slag fibers and is available in batt or rigid board form. It offers excellent fire resistance and soundproofing properties, making it a versatile choice for both residential and commercial buildings.

5. **Cellulose:** Cellulose insulation is crafted from recycled paper products treated with flame-retardant chemicals. It is typically blown into wall cavities or applied as loose-fill insulation. Its eco-friendly nature and effectiveness in reducing heat transfer make it a sustainable option for many insulation projects.

6. **Spray Foam:** Spray polyurethane foam (SPF) is a versatile insulation material that expands upon application. It can effectively fill gaps, cracks, and difficult-to-reach areas, creating an airtight seal. SPF provides superior insulation and acts as an air and moisture barrier, enhancing energy efficiency.

7. **Rigid Foam:** Rigid foam boards, like expanded polystyrene (EPS) and extruded polystyrene (XPS), offer high insulation values and moisture resistance. These lightweight and durable materials are often used in insulating foundations, walls, and roofs, where moisture control is important.

8. **Reflective Insulation:** Reflective insulation utilizes shiny surfaces or coatings to reflect heat radiation away from a building. It is commonly used in attics and crawl spaces to reduce radiant heat gain, making it a suitable choice for hot climates where minimizing heat transfer is crucial.

The choice of insulation material depends on factors like tender item, cost, desired R-value, available space, moisture resistance, fire safety, and local building codes. Insulation is typically installed during construction or added later as an improvement measure. It plays a crucial role in reducing energy consumption, greenhouse gas emissions, and the overall environmental impact of buildings.

Chapter 4

EXAMPLES OF INSULATING MATERIALS FOR ECO-FRIENDLY BUILDINGS

Eco-friendly buildings place a strong emphasis on sustainability, energy efficiency, and the use of environmentally responsible materials. In this chapter, we explore various insulating materials that align with these principles, providing effective insulation while minimizing the environmental impact. We will focus on three categories of insulating materials: mineral insulation, synthetic insulation, and animal and vegetable-based insulation, highlighting their eco-friendly features and applications in sustainable construction. Insulation materials are the key point to ensure thermal comfort. They have to be correctly chosen, depending on our needs, and our will to limit our impact on the environment. They can be of different kinds: mineral, synthetic or animal and vegetable-based.

The following tables explain how the materials presented are manufactured, their thermal conductivity, their general properties and their conditions of use.

(Courtesy - https://www.ecopassivehouses.com)

Mineral insulation

Mineral insulation materials are renowned for their eco-friendly properties, as they are made from naturally occurring minerals and recycled materials. Two common types in this category are rock wool and slag wool insulation.

- **Rock Wool Insulation:** Rock wool is made from basalt rock, a volcanic material, and typically contains recycled steel slag. It offers excellent fire resistance and soundproofing capabilities, making it a top choice for eco-conscious builders. It is used in various applications, such as wall insulation, sound barriers, and fire-resistant barriers.

- **Slag Wool Insulation:** Slag wool insulation is derived from blast furnace slag, a byproduct of the steel industry. It is a highly sustainable option, as it repurposes waste materials. Slag wool insulation is used in similar applications as rock wool and is known for its fire-resistant properties.

- **Aerogel Insulation:** This super-light, porous material is great for high-performance insulation. It's eco-friendly because it's made from silica gel, which is safe and efficient.

EXAMPLES OF INSULATING MATERIALS FOR ECO-FRIENDLY BUILDINGS

Mterils	Picture	Manufacturing	Thermal conductivity (W/m. K)	Properties	Conditions of use
Foam glass		Sand/limestone	0,038 to 0.055	- Non-combustible - Resistant to T°C > 430°C - Waterproof - Dimensional stability - Resistant to rodents, Insects, acids	Suitable for flat roofs, walls, foundations Available in sheets, panels or granules Not recommended for irregular surfaces
Glass wool		Silica and glass recovered by melting, then fibering and polymerization	0.03 to 0.04	- Resists up to 260°C - Non-flammable in the presence of a vapour barrier - Resistant to rodents - Root proof but blows over when humid	Suitable for sloping roofs, attics, wall partitions, cellings Available in semi-rigid panels, flakes or rolls Wearing gloves and glasses
Rock wool		Basalt, fondant and coke	0.032 to 0.04	- Fire, heat resistant - Excellent compressive strength - Moisture resistant and vapour permeable (possibility of respiratory discomfort)	Suitable for sloping roofs, attics, walls, cellings Available in semi-rigid panels, flakes or rolls Wearing gloves and glasses
Perlite		Volcanic silica rock crushed and heated to 12000C	0.05 to 0.06	- Hydrophilic (so it must be combined with a water repellent) - Durable and ecological but expensive -High compressive strength - Effective against bacteria, rodents - Non-combustible	Suitable for cellings, roofs and attics Available in panels or granules
Varmiculite		Magnesium silicate, a natural and abundant resource	0.06 to 0.08	- Expanded under the action of extreme heat (1000°C) or water vappour => water repelient treatment required - Non-combustible and rotproof - Not imitating - Resistant to rodents/ insects - Good mechanical resistance	Suitable for attics and roofs Available in bulk or in panels
Expanded clay		Raw dried clay, reduced to flour, mixed with water and then heated	0.10 to 0.16	-Non-combustible and fire-resistant -Permeable to steam and water resistant but must dry to regain its properties -Rot-proof and resistant to corrosive/insect products	Available in bulk in granules and bead-based bull blocks

Synthetic insulation

The majority of those materials are coming from fossil resources. While some synthetic insulation materials may not be as environmentally friendly as mineral or natural alternatives, some eco-conscious options are available within this category. One such material is recycled PET (rPET) insulation.

- **Recycled PET (rPET) Insulation:** Recycled PET insulation is made from post-consumer plastic bottles that have been cleaned and processed into fiber. This eco-friendly choice reduces plastic waste and provides excellent thermal performance. rPET insulation is often used in applications like wall and ceiling insulation, contributing to a circular economy by reusing plastic waste.

- **Polystyrene Insulation (XPS and EPS):**

  1. **Extruded Polystyrene (XPS):** XPS insulation is a closed-cell, rigid foam board that provides high thermal resistance. It is often used for foundations, walls, and roofs and is moisture-resistant.

  2. **Expanded Polystyrene (EPS):** EPS insulation is a lightweight, versatile material available in various forms, including boards and beads. It is commonly used for wall insulation and can be used in combination with other materials.

- **Polyisocyanurate (Polyiso) Insulation:** Polyiso insulation is a type of foam board insulation that offers excellent thermal performance and is often used in roofing and wall applications. It is known for its high R-value and moisture resistance.

EXAMPLES OF INSULATING MATERIALS FOR ECO-FRIENDLY BUILDINGS

Mterils	Picture	Manufacturing	Thermal conductivity (W/m. K)	Properties	Conditions of use
Expnded Polystyrene (EPS)		Crude oilo - blls compression-bonded during molding	0.029-0.038	- Fragile in the face of fire: requires associating it with plaster, for example - Releases CO_2, H_2O nd CO in case of fire - Unstable over time -Sensitive to the action of corrosives and rodents	Recommended on regular surfaces for roof, wall and floor indulation In the form of plates
Extruded Polystyrene (XPS)		Crude oid - balls compression-bonded during molding	0.029-0.037	- Compression-resistant - Waterproof, cold, heat resistant - Fragile in the face of fire (combine it with plaster)	Basements, flat roofs, floors, heated underfloor, double walls Panels with smooth or flush edges
Polyurethane (PUR)		Polyurethanes are produced by the reaction of an isocyanate and a polyol of various types	0,022-0,030	- Good compression support - Moisture does not alter it - Micro-porosity of its structure: allows water vapour to migrate from the inside to the outside => no need for a vapour barrier - Dangerous in case of fire: releases toxic gases	Roofs, flat roofs, floors, wall lining Suitable for renovation and construction Foams or panels
Phenolic foam		Phenol-formaldehyde resign	0,018-0,035	- Fireproof and low smoke emission during combustion - Sensitive to mosture: requires water repellent	Roofs, walls, floors Panels
Thin insulating		Lightweight and thin material Aluminum layers + other layers (felt, wadding, foam…) => multi-layer or reflective insulation	0,1-1 Prevents heat losses	- Lightweight - Low thickness - No health risk - Water vapour tight	Handy, Flesible On all surfaces Not irriating to the skin, so wearing a glove is not necessary
Vacuum insulating panels (VIP)		Composed of a central material (= aerogesls) confined in a sealed film and placed in a vacuum	0,0042-0,0050 cm VIP = 6 cm EPS and 9 cm of mineral wool	- Water vapour permeable (Installtion of a vapour barrier recommended) - Good compressive strength	Suitable for flat surfaces Disadvantage: must not be drilled and the panells cannot be cut out

Mterils	Picture	Manufacturing	Thermal conductivity (W/m. K)	Properties	Conditions of use
Aerogel		Nanotechnologies Composed of 99.8% air	0,011-0,013 Three times more insulating than glass wool	- Resistnt to T°C > 2000°C - Water vapour permeable (combine with a vapour barrier) - Compressive strength and can support 2000 times its weight	Reuires protective euipment
Insulating paint		Initially used on space shuttles Water-based acrylic paint - low VOC content	0,55	- Weather, mould and dirt resistant	Cold room, air-conditioned rooms facades, roofs On all types of substrates: concrete, wood, metal, PVC...
Block in clay		Produced from soil and water at high temperture. It contains a large amount of air.	0,12-0,18 and can reach lower value as 0,07 if cells filled with rock wool	- Good fire, rodent and water resistance - Does not release toxic substances	Very easy to install and saves time compared to conventional construction Naturally insulating.
Blocmonomur en pierre ponce		Porous volcanic stone, low density. Bound to cement gives monomer blocks	0,09-0,12	- Used to build breathable walls - Not very sensitive to rising dampness from the ground (low capillarity) - Resistance to fire, insects and rodents	Traditional way either by filling the joints or by gluing
Block in expanded clay		Blocks made from expanded clay beads, fired, sized and mixed with cement	0.11	- Non-combustible, durable over time - Resistant to insects and rodents - Water resistant	Easy to use
Porous concrete		Silliceous sand + cement + lime + aluminium powder (trapped air)	0,09	- Hydrophilic: must be protected from water by a special external coating - Good fire resistance, insects and rodents - Good compressive strength	In the form of single wall blocks, slabs, partitions and special blocks

Animal and vegetable-based insulation

Insulation materials derived from animals and plants are gaining popularity in eco-friendly construction due to their sustainability, biodegradability, and low environmental impact. Some examples of these insulating materials include sheep's wool, cotton, and hemp.

- **Sheep's Wool Insulation:** Sheep's wool insulation is made from the fleece of sheep, which is a renewable resource. It is known for its excellent thermal properties, moisture regulation, and fire resistance. Sheep's wool insulation is often used in residential and commercial buildings, providing natural insulation with minimal environmental impact.

- **Cotton Insulation:** Cotton insulation is composed of recycled denim or cotton fibers, making it an eco-friendly choice. It is free from chemical irritants and has good soundproofing qualities. Cotton insulation is suitable for wall and ceiling applications in residential and commercial structures.

- **Bamboo Insulation:** Bamboo insulation is an emerging eco-friendly material derived from the fast-growing bamboo plant. It is a renewable resource that requires minimal water and pesticides for cultivation. Bamboo insulation is naturally mold-resistant, provides good thermal performance, and is suitable for various building applications, contributing to sustainable construction practices.

BLUEPRINT FOR ENERGY EFFICIENT BUILDINGS

Mterils	Picture	Manufacturing	Thermal conductivity (W/m. K)	Properties	Conditions of use
Cork		Made of cork and 96% air	0,032-0,049 depending on packaging Good thermal shift	- Resists to compaction - Stable against differences in humidity and T°C - Rot proof - Self-extingushing (burns on contact with a flame but extinguishes on its own when removed) - Does not emit toxic fumes - Not attacked by rodents and insects	Expanded cork available in plates or in bulk (granules) Agglomerated cork available in plates, slabs and rolls Reuired thickness from 20 to 100 mm
Wood fiber (wool wood)		Obtained from the defibration of fire scraps.	0,037-0,049 Good thermal shift	- Ageing very well - Low flammability - Does not emit toxic fumes - Hygroscopic = can store moisture - Cleanses the air in the house and regulates humidity	Available in rigid or semi-rigid panels and in bulk Panels: exterior roof insulation, slabs and floors, exterior walls under cladding, wood framing, interior walls and partitions Bulk: empty filling of stoping roofs, partitions and floors
Hemp		Made from natural fibers from the fibrous part of the hemp tree	0,04-0,046	- Rot proof - Anti-fungal - Antibacterial - Resistance to insects and rodents - No chemical toxicity - Flammable - Addition of synthetic binders necessary to guarantee its resistance over time	Suitable for walls, roofs, attics, partitions Avilable in panels, rolls, mattresses or in bulk
Linen		Made from linen fibers too short to be used in the textile industry	0,037-0,040	- Very good longevity - Impregnated with boron salt to resist mould, insects and fire - May blow over - Rot proof - Ability to absorb and release mosture	Suitable for insulating walls, roofs, floors, attics Available in panels, rolls, bulk or felt
Sheep's wool		After mowing: soaking, degreasing, rinsing, treatments + boron salt to protect against fire, moulds and insects + moth control treatment	0,035-0,042	- Low flammability and tends to self-extinguish - Vertical settlement - Not suitable for wet areas	Suitable for roofs or attics Available in bulk, rolls, felt
Wool based on duck feathers		Made of 70% duck feathers and other binders (polyester fibers, sheep wool...)	0,33-0,42	- Permeable to water vapour but retains insulating properties after drying - Treatment allows it to resist fungi and insects - Possible settlement	Suitable for attic spaces, separately applied cellings, walls, wooden frame houses, floating floors Available in rolls and panels

EXAMPLES OF INSULATING MATERIALS FOR ECO-FRIENDLY BUILDINGS

Mterils	Picture	Manufacturing	Thermal conductivity (W/m. K)	Properties	Conditions of use
Coconut fibres		Brown coconut fibre from ripe coconuts and white from green coconuts	0,037-0,045	- Rot proof - Does not fear fungi or insects - Moisture resistant -Dries quickly - Good dimensional stability	Suitble for floors, patitions, roofs Available in bulk, panels, rolls, felts
Reeds panels		Brown coconut fibre from ripe coconuts and white from green coconuts	0,037-0,045	- Rot proof - Does not fear funge or insects - Moisture resistant - Dries quickly - Good dimensional stability	Suitable for floors, partitions, roofs Available in bulk, panels, rolls, felts
Cellulose wadding		Reeds ssembled with good glvniezed wire	0,056	- Low flammability - Does not emit any smoke	For external thermal insultion. verticl or creeping walls and on roofs Panels or mesh Attached with screws or nails
Cotton wool		Natural and recycled cotton from cut and clothing waste	0,037-0,042	- Very permeble to water vapour = good hygrometric regulator - Treated aginst insect and fungi + boron salt to make it fire resistant - Can settle down - Not sensitive to moisture	Suitable for attics, building voids, walls, roofs and floors In bulk, in rolls, in felt and in sheets A lot of dus so wear flasses and mask
Straw		Stem resulting from the production of cereal grains (wheat, barley, oats, rye, rice) cut aut at harvest.	0,05-0,075	- Thermoregulatory material - Good durability, good mechanical resistance - Good hygrometric regulator - Flammable and thereforenecessary to be accompanied by a facing - Precautions to be taken to protect from soil moisture and rodents	Bales Building blocks or bulk Suitable for floors, attics, building voids. Used to fill wooden ame walls ==> very good passive type insulation External insulation (only for self builders because no technical advice is required)
Cob		Straw + water + clay or soil mixture – low-insulation plasters	Must be used in addition to an other material 0,57-0,59	- Good durability - Absorbs moisture and makes habitat breathe	For filling wooden frames, floors, walls or on wooden slats On a slightly damp surface for better adhesion For better insulation: increase the straw content For better thermal inertia: increase the proportion of soil

Green roof		Usually consists of: - the support element - an insulating material - a vapour barrier - an insulating material - a waterproof coating - draining layer and a filtering layer - of a culture and vegetation	Used to complete the insulation of a home. Allows to reduce by 40% the variations of T°C	Good longevity if project well designed	Thick ground mats + mixed and rooted plants (on solid framework) on intermediate layer (wooden files or plastic tarpaulins) Types of plantations: intensive, semi-extensive and extensive.

You can also check more information on ECBC 2017 codes:

https://beeindia.gov.in/sites/default/files/BEE_ECBC%202017.pdf

Chapter 5

INSULATION INSTALLATION TIPS & BEST PRACTICES

Proper insulation installation is essential to maximize the benefits of insulation materials, whether it's for thermal performance, energy efficiency, or soundproofing. In this chapter, we will discuss important tips and best practices for the successful installation of insulation in various building applications. Following these guidelines ensures that insulation performs optimally and provides long-lasting benefits.

Pre-Installation Preparation:

Pre-installation preparation means getting ready before you put insulation in a building. It's like making sure you have all the ingredients before you start cooking. Before starting the insulation installation, there are several key preparatory steps to consider:

- **Assess the Building Envelope:** Carefully examine the building's structure to identify areas that require insulation. This includes walls, ceilings, floors, and any potential air gaps, cracks, or voids.

- **Choose the Right Insulation Material:** Select the appropriate insulation material based on the specific application and local climate conditions. Ensure that the material's R-value matches the insulation needs of the area.

- **Safety Precautions:** Take safety precautions, including wearing appropriate personal protective equipment (PPE) like gloves, masks, and eye protection when working with insulation materials that may cause skin irritation or dust.

Installation Techniques:

Installation techniques are like the steps and methods you follow to put insulation in a building properly. It's a bit like following a recipe to cook a meal. Effective installation techniques are crucial for achieving the desired insulation performance:

- **Seal Air Leaks:** Prioritize air sealing to prevent drafts and heat loss. Use caulk or expanding foam to seal gaps and cracks in the building envelope before installing insulation.

- **Moisture Control:** Ensure that the installation area is dry and free from moisture issues. Address any leaks or water intrusion problems before adding insulation.

- **Proper Placement:** Install insulation materials with consistent thickness and coverage. Avoid compressing insulation, as it reduces its effectiveness. Fill gaps and voids completely to minimize thermal bridging.

- **Cut and Fit:** Trim insulation materials accurately to fit around obstructions such as electrical wiring, plumbing, and framing. Maintain a tight fit without leaving gaps.

Safety and Health Considerations:

Safety and health considerations involve the guidelines and measures you should follow to protect yourself and maintain your well-being while working with insulation. It's similar to following safety practices in a workshop or laboratory to prevent accidents and maintain good health.

- **Respiratory Protection:** When working with loose-fill insulation or materials that produce dust, use a mask or respirator to protect your lungs from inhaling airborne particles.

- **Ventilation:** Ensure proper ventilation when working in enclosed spaces to disperse any fumes or dust generated during insulation installation.

- **Avoid Skin Contact:** Some insulation materials can be irritating to the skin. Wear long-sleeved clothing and gloves to protect your skin from contact.

Quality Control and Inspection:

Quality control and inspection involve carefully reviewing and evaluating the work to ensure it meets the required standards and is error-free. After completing the insulation installation, conduct a thorough quality control check:

- **Check for Gaps:** Inspect for gaps, voids, or areas with insufficient coverage. Fill any missed spots or gaps in the insulation.

- **Energy Audits:** Consider conducting an energy audit or thermal imaging assessment to verify the insulation's effectiveness and identify any remaining issues.

- **Fire Safety:** Ensure that insulation materials are installed with the proper fire protection measures in place, especially in areas where fire safety is a concern.

Proper insulation installation is a critical component of achieving energy efficiency, thermal comfort, and soundproofing in buildings. By following the tips and best practices outlined in this chapter, you can ensure that insulation materials are installed correctly and safely, maximizing their performance and contributing to a more sustainable and comfortable living or working environment. Insulation is an investment that pays off in the form of reduced energy bills and increased comfort when installed with care and attention to detail.

Chapter 6

ENERGY SAVINGS WITH INSULATION

In today's world, where environmental concerns and the rising cost of energy are becoming increasingly prominent, it is crucial to explore effective ways to reduce energy consumption and lower utility bills. One such method is insulation, a versatile and cost-effective approach to conserving energy in both residential and commercial buildings. With the ever-increasing cost of energy and the growing awareness of environmental issues, finding ways to reduce energy consumption and lower our carbon footprint is more important than ever. Insulation plays a central role in achieving these goals, offering a cost-effective and environmentally friendly solution to conserving energy in our homes and buildings. This chapter provides an overview of the importance of insulation and its significant role in achieving energy savings.

Energy Savings with Insulation

Insulation offers a wide range of benefits, with energy savings being one of the most significant advantages. Here's how proper insulation can lead to substantial reductions in your energy bills:

Reduced Heating and Cooling Costs

Properly insulated homes and buildings are better at retaining the desired indoor temperature. During the winter, insulation prevents the loss of warm air, reducing the need for your heating system to work constantly. In the summer, it keeps your home cooler by preventing excess heat from entering. As a result, you'll rely less on your air conditioner, leading to lower energy bills.

Increased Comfort

Good insulation creates a more stable indoor climate, with fewer temperature fluctuations. This means you won't have to constantly adjust your thermostat to maintain comfort. You'll experience fewer cold drafts in the winter and less heat infiltration in the summer, creating a more pleasant living or working environment.

Extended Lifespan of HVAC Systems

Since your heating and cooling systems won't need to run as frequently or work as hard, insulation can help extend the lifespan of these expensive appliances. Reduced wear and tear means you'll save not only on energy bills but also on repair and replacement costs over time.

Environmental Benefits

Energy savings with insulation aren't just about your wallet; they're also about the planet. By using less energy to heat and cool your home, you reduce your carbon footprint and help mitigate the effects of climate change. Lower energy consumption means fewer greenhouse gas emissions, making your home more eco-friendly.

Proper Insulation Installation

To maximize energy savings, it's essential to ensure that insulation is installed correctly. Inadequate insulation, gaps, and compression can diminish its effectiveness. It's recommended to consult with a professional insulation contractor who can assess your specific needs and install the right type and amount of insulation in the proper locations.

Insulation is a key player in energy efficiency and energy savings. By creating a thermal barrier between your indoor environment and the outside world, insulation helps you maintain a comfortable temperature, reduce heating and cooling costs, and contribute to a greener planet. When it comes to sustainable living and economic savings, insulation is an investment that pays significant dividends for both your wallet and the environment.

Some simple energy-saving tips and tricks:

1. **Insulate Exterior Walls:** Adding insulation to exterior walls can significantly improve your home's energy efficiency. This may involve wall cavity insulation or external cladding.

2. **Insulate Floors:** If you have an unheated or uninsulated crawl space or basement beneath your home, insulating the floors above can prevent heat loss and make your living space more comfortable.

3. **Install Roof Insulation:** A well-insulated roof can make a substantial difference in your energy bills. Consider adding insulation to the roof or attic space.

4. **Choose Energy-Efficient Doors:** When replacing exterior doors, opt for energy-efficient options with a solid core and good insulation properties.

5. **Use Draft Stoppers:** Place draft stoppers at the bottom of exterior doors to prevent cold air from seeping in during the winter.

6. **Use Insulated Curtains:** Install thermal or insulated curtains on windows to reduce heat transfer and maintain a comfortable indoor temperature.

7. **Insulate your Water Heater:** Insulating your water heater tank and pipes can reduce heat loss, which means your water heater won't have to work as hard to maintain hot water temperatures.

8. **Maintain Existing Insulation:** Regularly inspect existing insulation for signs of damage or compression. Replace or repair insulation as needed to maintain its effectiveness.

9. **Upgrade to Energy-Efficient Appliances:** Consider replacing old and inefficient appliances with energy-efficient models, which can reduce the heat load on your home.

10. **Use Natural Light:** During the day, rely on natural daylight to reduce the need for artificial lighting and associated heat generation.

Chapter 7

ADVANCED INSULATION APPLICATIONS

In the pursuit of energy efficiency and sustainability, advanced insulation applications have emerged as cutting-edge solutions that go beyond traditional insulation materials and methods. These innovative techniques and materials offer improved thermal performance, durability, and environmental benefits.

As we search for ways to save energy and protect the planet, some exciting new ideas have emerged to keep our homes and buildings comfy. These creative methods and materials go beyond the basics and bring us improved warmth, lasting strength, and a cleaner environment. In this chapter, we'll take a closer look at these cool ways to insulate our spaces.

Aerogel Insulation

Aerogel, often referred to as "frozen smoke," is a remarkable material with one of the lowest thermal conductivities of any known substance. It consists of a solid network of interconnected silica nanoparticles, making it incredibly lightweight. This makes aerogel insulation an ideal choice for applications where space is limited, such as insulating spacecraft or high-performance buildings.

The key benefits of aerogel insulation include:

- Exceptional thermal resistance.

- Ultra-lightweight, reducing structural load.

- Thin profile, allowing for more space in constrained environments.

- Resistance to moisture and fire.

- Sustainable and eco-friendly.

Vacuum Insulation Panels (VIPs)

Vacuum insulation panels are high-performance, thin insulation materials that rely on a vacuum-sealed core to reduce thermal conductivity. These panels consist of a core material, such as fiberglass or foam, enclosed in an airtight envelope. The removal of air from within the panel eliminates heat transfer through conduction and convection, resulting in outstanding insulation properties.

The advantages of VIPs include:

- Superb insulating capabilities in a compact form.

- Suitable for retrofitting into existing buildings.

- Long-lasting performance with minimal thickness.

- Ideal for applications with limited space.

Phase Change Materials (PCMs)

Phase change materials are substances that can absorb and release thermal energy as they change from a solid to a liquid or vice versa. When incorporated into building materials or insulation, PCMs can help regulate indoor temperatures by absorbing excess heat during the day and releasing it at night.

Key features of PCM-based insulation include:

- Improved thermal mass for temperature stability.
- Reduced reliance on HVAC systems.
- Enhanced occupant comfort.
- Energy savings and reduced peak energy demand.

Smart Insulation

The emergence of smart materials and technology has led to the development of smart insulation systems. These systems use sensors, actuators, and control systems to adapt and optimize insulation performance in real-time. For example, dynamic insulation can change its thermal resistance based on the external temperature, reducing the need for active heating or cooling. The benefits of smart insulation include:

- Adaptive thermal control for maximum energy efficiency.
- Potential for integration with building management systems.
- Reduced energy consumption and operating costs.
- Improved comfort and indoor air quality.

Sustainable Insulation

The demand for sustainable building materials has driven the development of eco-friendly insulation options. Materials like recycled denim, cork, and natural fibers offer excellent thermal performance while minimizing the environmental impact. These materials are often sourced from renewable resources or recycled content.

The advantages of sustainable insulation include:

- Reduced environmental footprint.
- Low embodied energy.
- Healthier indoor air quality.
- Recycling and renewable resource support.

Insulated Concrete Forms (ICFs)

ICFs are a construction technique that combines insulation with the structural elements of a building. They consist of hollow blocks or forms made from materials like expanded polystyrene (EPS) or foam. These forms are stacked, reinforced with steel, and filled with concrete, creating a highly insulated and durable building envelope.
ICFs offer several benefits, including:

- High thermal performance and energy efficiency.
- Superior structural integrity and durability.
- Noise reduction.
- Resistance to extreme weather events.

Transparent Insulation

Transparent insulation materials have the unique property of allowing natural daylight to enter while providing insulation properties. Examples include vacuum glazing and aerogel glazing. These materials are used in windows and skylights to improve energy efficiency while maintaining a connection to the outdoors. The advantages of transparent insulation include:

- Daylight harvesting for reduced lighting needs.
- Reduced solar heat gain.
- Improved thermal comfort.

Cool Roofs

Cool roofs are designed to reflect more sunlight and absorb less heat than standard roofs. They are typically coated with reflective materials and come in various forms, including cool roofing shingles and coatings. Cool roofs can significantly reduce a building's cooling load and lower indoor temperatures.

Key benefits of cool roofs include:

- Reduced energy consumption for air conditioning.

- Lower urban heat island effect.

- Extended roof lifespan.

- Enhanced occupant comfort.

Radiant Barrier Insulation

Radiant barrier insulation reflects radiant heat, such as the heat from the sun, away from the building. It consists of a highly reflective material, often applied to the underside of the roof, attic floor, or walls. By reducing radiant heat gain, it can keep buildings cool in hot climates and reduce air conditioning costs.

The advantages of radiant barrier insulation include:

- Effective in hot climates with strong sun exposure.

- Improved comfort in upper floors and attics.

- Energy savings and reduced cooling costs.

Advanced Installation Techniques

Apart from fancy insulation stuff, there are smart ways to make our buildings cozy. These methods involve sealing gaps and cracks, making everything airtight, and using special tools like heat-sensing cameras to make sure our insulation does its job really well.

So, to sum it up, the cool new insulation ideas are making our buildings more energy-efficient and eco-friendly. They help keep us comfy, save the Earth, and as time goes on, we'll come up with even better ways to do it. It's like finding new superhero powers for our homes and buildings to fight energy waste and environmental problems.

CASE STUDY

Let's go through the case study of Mr. Aditya Gupta, a man who is building his dream four-story house in a posh area of Delhi. Aditya is determined to create a remarkable home and seeks advice from architects and industry experts on every aspect, from the structure to the interiors. However, there is one crucial detail no one mentions: how to save energy and make the building more comfortable with insulation.

Unaware of this missing piece, Aditya follows the crowd and opts for a brick bat coba on his roof, as many others do. Little does he know that in the scorching summers of North India, the atmospheric temperatures soar to a blistering 45 degrees Celsius, and the surface temperature reaches a staggering 60 degrees. It's in these extreme conditions that Aditya begins to feel the heavy burden of not consulting an insulation expert.

Even with the air conditioners running all day, his house remains uncomfortably hot, and Aditya grows frustrated with the situation. That's when a common friend suggested that he consult me. After understanding Aditya's requirements and assessing the building's construction, I recommended a solution: applying Spray Polyurethane Foam (PUF) insulation on the roof as a sandwich system and using insulation boards on the exterior walls or a high Solar Reflective Index (SRI) coating.

Aditya wastes no time in accepting my suggestion and proceeds with the recommended insulation method. Once the work is completed, a wave of relief washes over him. In the first month after the insulation is executed, Aditya notices a dramatic decrease in the temperature inside his home and a 40% reduction in his energy bills. Overjoyed by the results, he becomes a passionate advocate for using insulation in both new and existing constructions. Sadly, the only regret in this entire case study is that if Aditya had known about insulation or sought advice from an insulation expert earlier, he could have saved the additional expense of dismantling the roof and implementing the insulation solution.

RETURN ON INVESTMENT

Now, let's talk about the most crucial part of insulation: "Return on Investment" (ROI). Insulation not only creates comfort inside a building but also plays a significant role in reducing energy bills. It not only recovers the initial investment within a few years of installation but also generates savings, continuing throughout the building's lifetime. Let's understand this with the help of the example below:

Initial cost of insulation: Rs 2,50,000 Annual energy cost before insulation: Rs 1,40,000 Annual energy cost after insulation: Rs 85,000 Expected lifespan of the insulation: 50 years

Calculation of ROI:

1. **Calculate the annual energy savings:** Annual energy cost before insulation - Annual energy cost after insulation. Annual energy savings = Rs 1,40,000 - Rs 85,000 = Rs 55,000 (These savings are based on the current unit rate, which may increase over the years.)

2. **Calculate the payback period:** Initial cost of insulation / Annual energy savings. Payback period = Rs 2,50,000 / Rs 55,000 = 4.5 years

3. **Calculate the ROI:** (Annual energy savings * Expected lifespan of insulation) - Initial Cost. ROI = (Rs 55,000 * 50) - Rs 2,50,000 = Rs 25,00,000/-

In this example, the Rs 2,50,000 investment in insulation yields annual energy savings of Rs 55,000. It takes 4.5 years to recover the initial cost, and the overall ROI for the insulation project is 11%. This means that over the expected lifespan of the insulation, the investment returns 11% of the initial cost annually in energy savings.

Keep in mind that this is a simplified example, and actual ROI may vary based on various factors such as energy costs, insulation quality, building size, and climate conditions. It's recommended to conduct a thorough analysis specific to your situation to determine the accurate ROI for an insulated building.

RECAP

This book breaks down insulation in an easy-to-understand way, covering these important points:

- **Importance of Insulation:** We explored the significance of insulation in buildings, highlighting its role in energy efficiency, comfort, and sustainability.

- **Types of Insulation in Indian Buildings:** We discussed various insulation types used in India, including Brick Bat Coba, Mud Phuska, Fiberglass, and more.

- **Eco-Friendly Insulating Materials:** We introduced eco-friendly insulation materials like mineral insulation, synthetic insulation, and natural options derived from animal and vegetable-based insulation.

- **Insulation Installation Tips & Best Practices:** Valuable advice is provided to ensure the proper installation of insulation materials, maximizing their effectiveness.

- **Energy Savings with Insulation & Tips:** We explored how insulation significantly reduces energy costs, and we offered tips to optimize your energy savings.

- **Advanced Insulation Applications:** Cutting-edge

techniques and materials, such as Aerogel Insulation & Vacuum Insulation Panels (VIPs), were discussed to showcase the future of energy-efficient buildings.

- **Case Study:** Mr. Aditya Gupta's experience showcases the real impact of insulation on comfort and energy bills.

- **Return on Investment:** We discussed how insulation not only pays for itself but continues to generate substantial savings, emphasizing the financial benefits of proper insulation.

With this knowledge, you're ready to make smart choices about insulation for your projects, whether it's about saving energy, staying comfy, or being environmentally friendly.

NEXT STEP

After reading this book, what are your thoughts on insulation? If you are planning to construct a new building or seeking a solution for an existing one, you have two options:

Option 1: With the knowledge shared in this book, you can choose to take on the task yourself.

OR

Option 2: Hire a professional like us who can understand your needs and provide an appropriate solution. Let's chat over coffee and take your next step to achieve amazing results!

With Regards,

Author Name: VISHAL RUSTAGI
Email ID: vishal@ptsplgroup.com